A NIGHT FOR THE SHEPHERDS

All scripture quotations, unless otherwise indicated are taken from the New King James Version. Copyright 1992 by Thomas Nelson, Inc. All rights reserved.

Cover Image credit: Canva

Cover page design: Author

For feedback or any communication with the author, kindly send a mail to: naamhglobal@gmail.com

A NOTE TO THE READER

In your hand is a book about Jesus – not just Jesus the Saviour, but Jesus the Good Shepherd, who desires to guide us through the path of His purpose. As you turn the pages to carefully assimilate and ponder on the collection of words therein, may you find grace through the help of the Holy Spirit to live purposefully in following, beholding and reflecting Jesus.

And if you are yet to believe in Jesus for your salvation and accept Him as your Lord and Saviour, here's another opportunity to do so. You are the reason He went to the cross and rose the third day. He is the real essence of a purposeful and fulfilling life. He loves you; He really does.

GRACE

<u>PROLOGUE</u>

The brilliance of the early morning sunlight sparkled through the reflective screen of the bright sky. The charm of the colourful birds hugged the luscency of the delightful breeze for an indelible waltz of celebration. In the heart of a little town, a young shepherd nutured a sheepfold with passion, purpose and precision.

But David occassionally went and returned from Saul to feed his father's sheep at Bethlehem

But David said to Saul, "Your servant used to keep his father's sheep, and when a lion or a bear came and took a lamb out of the flock,

I went out after it and struck it, and delivered the lamb from its mouth; and when it arose against me, I caught it by its beard, and struck and killed it.

(1 Samuel 17:15, 34, 35).

In his quiet moments of tendering the sheepfold, David found God and in relating with Him, knew Him as his Shepherd. He would later pen down the words of Psalm 23 to express his experience of God's goodness and Jesus, many years after would introduce Himself as our good Shepherd (John 10:11). David mirrored in physical reality, what Jesus came to do in our spiritual reality. Hungry lion. Aggressive bear. Vulnerable lamb. Intentional David. Just like David rescued the lamb from the grip of the lion and the paws of the bear, Jesus snatched us eternally from the fangs of sin and death. Shepherds care for their sheep and put their lives on the line for them. Shepherds lead, guide, protect, provide for and promote the interests of the sheepfold.

Beyond all these, our good Shepherd chose to walk in the dark hallway of death to redeem us to His righteousness so we can walk with Him in peace, purpose and progress.

Therefore we were buried with Him through baptism into death, that just as Christ was raised by the glory of the Father, even so we should walk in newness of life (Romans 6:4).

Walking in the newness of life or in the real sense, walking in the newness of the life of Christ requires we walk with Him in obedience, honour and dignity, even as we totally depend on Him for every move. In this is the essence of the victorious and supernatural life we have been called into in Christ – the purpose of our rebirth into the eternal kingdom of God.

Seems like Bethlehem is a breeding spot for Shepherds. In it, David, a shepherd boy discovered God as his Shepherd and in it, our Lord and Saviour, our good Shepherd was born as a man to redeem us back to Himself.

Can we turn the page as we explore the guidance of our good Shepherd?

INTRODUCTION

Different seasons and events are celebrated globally and annually. Every 7th April is the World Health Organization's (WHO) day. On this day, a central theme is announced which would be the watch word for the year. May 1 is the day workers sing a song of rest and rejoice for being on a job. May 27 is the Children's day and December 1 is the World AIDS day. On December 25, we celebrate the birth of our Lord and Saviour Jesus Christ.

And have you ever wondered why the Christmas season seems unique and different from other seasons in the world? The Christmas songs. The Christmas trees. The Christmas lights. The traditional red and green ribbons. And what about the greetings, gifts, grandeur and glamour? But beyond all these, one important factor still distinguishes the Christmas season from others in the world. A brain teaser of some kind? You won't have to stretch your nerves beyond the limits. The answer is in the word 'CHRISTMAS'. Unlike other seasons in which there's an annual change in central themes, the focus of the season has remained the same – the Christ. The focal point of every Christmas is the Christ in the mass, and yes the mass in the Christ.

Let's not get it twisted. The world still celebrates the mass without the Christ, but that is like rejoicing over a car without an engine. And whoever wants to lie under a tree in the rain? Christ is the all-time reason for all seasons. He is the hub of the evangel. *All things were created through Him and for Him* (Colossians 1:16). It is through Him, by Him, in Him and for Him that we live.

Besides, other seasons celebrated in the world are usually focused on some particular set of people. May 1 is for workers, May 27 for children and April 7 for international health. Now, you can take a stroll on a lane in my heart as you think out the next statement. Christmas is celebrated all over the world and by all people from all walks of life. The young and the old. The rich and the poor. The sick and the healthy. The maimed and the whole. The Europeans, Asians, Hispanics and Africans. The professionals and the artisans.

Then the angel said to them, "Do not be afraid, for behold,

I bring you good tidings of great joy which will be to all

people (Luke 1:10).

The coming of Christ into the world is the good tiding of great joy to all people. The gospel of Christ is the Father's good news to a struggling world. Here in is the good news: because of what the Father did for us on the cross in Christ Jesus, we are totally disengaged from the sinful nature and are eternally united with Him in life, love and righteousness if we believe in Him and continue to do so. Imagine a world without Christ. It would have been a world where the inhabitants would have their lives futile because their minds would be darkened. It would have been a world without hope and with no vision for life. It would have been a world with no amazing insight for living and a world without the nature of God's righteousness. And so Jesus came and we have a different story to tell. To the hopeless, Jesus offers hope. To those without vision for life, Jesus offers the purpose for living. To the sinful, He offers forgiveness. To the timid, He offers boldness and confidence. To the weak, he provides strength. To the pessimist, he blows the wind of change. And to the self-righteous, He offers a new label – the righteousness of God.

The thief does not come, except to steal, and to kill and to destroy. I have come that they may have life, and that they may have it more abundantly (John 10:10).

We experience abundant life in Him as we nurture a progressive walking and talking relationship with Him.

This book is about insights from the events surrounding the birth of our Lord and Saviour Jesus Christ, His role in our lives as our good shepherd and how we can apply them in living the victorious life He has called us into in this present age. And we'd realize that even though the Christmas season is in December every year, for us who believe in Christ, every day is a Christmas day because Christ should be seen, celebrated and glorified in our daily decisions, intentions, actions, attitudes and characters.

CHAPTER 1

IN THE EYES OF THE GAME

Driving uphill can be a daunting task. Apart from slowing down the pace of a journey, it gives an expressionless pressure that robs of the pleasure of seeing what's ahead. We all love the treasure embellished in the desire of seeing what lies ahead. So was this peculiar damsel.

She was young, responsible and resourceful. If chastity was measured in pounds, hers would display 'unrecordable' on the scale. Her innocence was like a glow worm in the darkness of the night and her charm like the dew of a dawn – noticeable. She loved life and was full of it. The song of her purpose daily begged to be heard and on a fateful day, the wind of assurance blew over her heart.

Now in the sixth month the angel Gabriel was sent by God to a city of Galilee named Nazareth,

To a virgin betrothed to a man whose name was Joseph, of the house of David. The virgin's name was Mary.

And having come in, the angel said to her, "Rejoice, highly favored one, the Lord is with you; blessed are you among women!"

But when she saw him, she was troubled at his saying, and considered what manner of greeting this was.

Then the angel said to her, "Do not be afraid, Mary for you have found favor with God.

"And behold, you will conceive in your womb and bring forth a Son and shall call His name JESUS.

"He will be great, and will be called the Son of the Highest; and the Lord God will give Him the throne of His Father David.

"And He will reign over the house of Jacob forever, and of His kingdom there will be no end."

Then Mary said to the angel, "How can this be, since I do not know a man?"

And the angel answered and said to her, "The Holy Spirit will come upon you, and the power of the Highest will overshadow you; therefore, also, that Holy One who is to be born will be called the Son of God.

"Now indeed, Elizabeth your relative has also conceived a son in her old age; and this is now the sixth month for her who was called barren.

"For with God nothing will be impossible."

Then Mary said, "Behold the maidservant of the Lord! Let it be to me according to your word." And the angel departed from her (Luke 1:26-38).

Confused and dumbfounded. Afraid and hyper alert. Skeptical and critical. Mary did not only get a vision for her life, but also moved through the usual process of acceptance of a vision (from the Lord). Before continuing with Mary's story, let's pitch a tent with the word 'vision'. Vision is the sight of God's purpose for our lives with the eyes of our minds. Purpose is the reason God created us and for which he has put us here on earth.

A cast of characters and a quick profile of their lives may be useful here:

Abraham was to be a father of many nations.

Joseph was framed by God to be a godly ruler.

Nehemiah was picked by God to rebuild the walls of Jerusalem.

Esther was designed to be a Queen to rescue God's people.

Samuel declared God's word as a prophet in Israel.

For Mary, it was to give birth to the Messiah.

Luke was a Medical Doctor and a Christian writer.

Apostle Paul preached the message of the cross to the Gentiles.

Now, did you notice a pattern here? Let me whisper this into your ears: living for the purpose for which God created us on earth is not the pursuit of some selfish and personal ambitions. Because it is God's purpose, it must be God-ordained, God-defined and God-directed. Whether it is to create and grow a business, invent an entity, build a school, pursue a career, care for the aged or the orphans, preach to prisoners, pastor a church, establish a church-based ministry or volunteer for an existing one; it must be God-defined and of His kingdom relevance.

The presence of a grossly thick cloud is a tell-tale sign that a heavy downpour is near. Strong steps of gold. Bright waves of silver. I know the next line in your thought is "how do I know God's purpose for my life?"; simple!

1. Be born again and be passionate about knowing and following God's will for your life through ardent studying of His word and prayers.

2. Ask God to let you know His purpose for your life. Instead of a long shopping list of some perishable goods that we take to God's presence, one great request that God will gladly attend to is the issue of His purpose for our lives. "Ask, and it will be given to you; seek, and you will find; knock, and it will be opened to you (Matthew 7:7).

3. Develop a well-cultivated walking and talking relationship with God. But as it is written: "Eye has not seen, nor ear heard, Nor have entered into the heart of man the things which God has prepared for

those who love Him." But God has revealed them to us through His Spirit. For the Spirit searches all things, yes, the deep things of God. For what man knows the things of a man except the spirit of the man which is in him? Even so no one knows the things of God except the Spirit of God (1 Corinthians 2:9-11). So, one of the deep things of God is the revelation of His purpose for our lives.

4. Walk in the love of God

5. Use your gifts, talents and potentials to serve God because they are pointers to what God wants to do with your life. And in doing this, employ the acronym SWIPE.

S – Strength. You will have to locate your place of strength; that is what you know how to do well and effortlessly or the cultivation of spiritual gifts as we can only be excellent in the place of our strengths.

W – Weakness. It is good to identify and know the areas we are not good at so as to avoid being distracted by them, but if relevant for our purpose, we can work on them to bring out strengths from them (Hebrews 11:34).

I – Interests. What are the things that readily arouse your interest?

P – Personality. Your personality type may be relevant to your area of purpose.

E – Experiences. Just like your personality, your experiences may be linked to who you are called to be.

So, this is a little guide in knowing God's purpose for our lives, even as we totally submit to the

Lordship of our Saviour and the guidance of the Holy Spirit.

Do you remember how we got here? First, the angel Gabriel visited Mary. Then, Mary accepted his offer. Later on, we had a purposeful diversion. Why not let's go back to Mary's story? Mary was surprised, troubled and afraid at the sight of the angel and his greeting. And to calm her nerves, he offered her a tranquilizing dose of the treasures of God:

"Now indeed, Elizabeth your relative has also conceived a son in her old age; and this is now the sixth month for her who was called barren.

"For with God, nothing will be impossible" (Luke 1:36, 37).

Elizabeth's conception of a son at her old age was a proof that nothing is impossible with God and Mary needed to see that to be fully convinced of going for God's purpose for her life. God will go to any length to confirm the immutability of His counsel concerning His purpose for our lives, which He has eternally accomplished in Christ for us. And to do this, sometimes He shows us both biblical and contemporary examples of people who have achieved seemingly impossible feats for Him by their walk with and dependence on Him.

Do you walk the earth with Mary's shoes wondering why in the world God has put such a 'huge' and 'impossible' vision in your heart? The full dose of God's tranquilizer is still available: for with God (not with men, not with native intelligence, not with resume) nothing (that is no thing; not few things, not certain things) will be impossible (Luke 1:37, emphasis mine).

Another point to note is that age is not a determinant in the place of fulfilling God's purpose for our lives. Mary gave birth to God's purpose at a young age, Elizabeth did at an old age; but they both did. The key factor is following God and walking in His will for our lives. He has made everything beautiful in its time (Ecclesiastes 3:11).

CHAPTER 2

THE DRIFT OF THE GAME

The toddler and pre-school periods are strategic phases in

the growth of a child. Because of the continuous

processes of brain development, the fortitude of their

vocabularies intensifies as the glowing embers of their

interests in their environments beg to be seen. This was

particularly unfolded even in the life of the first toddler gifted to my wife and I. Jaden wanted me to help him with his homework and I wanted him to help me get an afternoon nap by being quiet. He came into the room struggling to hold his books, some of which were already torn. As he persisted with his golden request, his books slipped off his hands, got torn and were all scattered on the floor. Immediately, he attempted to pick them up, but the more he tried, the further they got torn. As I saw this, I told him to leave the books and that I'd help him pack them. "No, No…", he shouted amidst tears as though his entire life depends solely on what he could make happen by his ability at that moment.

Can you relate with this? I can. We all can. When certain parts of our lives seem to fall apart – when the visions in our hearts appear as illusions in reality; when the babies

do not come as expected; when the business seem to fail,
the interviews appear endless and even the job that
stayed is a miniature compared to the qualification. When
a flourishing career gets challenged or the seeds of
repeated attempts at an exam fail to yield the fruits of
successful celebration, our reasoning whisper to us that
our entire lives and future depend solely on those
moments and what we can make happen by our abilities.
We become control-freaks and with rods of frustration
and trepidation, we chase our little minds into a cage of
horror – worry. The more we try to 'help ourselves', the
deeper we sink into this hole. Planted in the pages of the
scriptures is a great survival skill Jesus emphasized when
He gloriously walked the sands of the earth. Matthew
takes the stage:

Therefore I say unto you, take no thought for your life, what you shall eat, or what you shall drink; nor yet for your body, what you shall put on. Is not the life more than meat, and the body than raiment?

Behold the fowls of the air: for they sow not, neither do they reap, nor gather into barns; yet your heavenly Father feeds them?

Which of you by taking thought can add one cubit unto his stature?

And why take you thought for raiment? Consider the lilies of the field, how they grow; they toil not, neither do they spin:

And yet I say unto you, that even Solomon in all his glory was not arrayed like one of these

Wherefore, if God so clothe the grass of the field, which today is, and tomorrow is cast into the oven, shall He not much more clothe you, O you of little faith (Matthew 6:25-30)

Widened eyes. Narrowed minds. Slippery feet. The listeners of Jesus' message must have put their minds to flight in amazement of what was sipping into the chambers of their ears. Eat. Body. Clothe. Do not worry? Does the Father care so much about the fine details of our lives? Does He care so much about our next meals, paychecks, business deals, medical bills and house rent? Yes, He does. And if He so cares about the little aspects of our lives, dare we think He would mishandle the greater aspects of our purpose (or better put, His purpose) and the great future ahead? The birds and the lilies live helplessly and our Father sees to their needs. When we worry, we wrongly affirm that our lives totally depend on us – what we do or what we don't do. This prevents us from going helpless before God to exchange our weaknesses for His strength.

Hey! Let's pause for a while and listen to the pulsating voice of one of our dear brethren (I hope this is not you). "So, does it mean Jesus is saying we should have no plan and live carelessly because He cares for us?" (Did you actually think that out?) Jesus did not mean we should be careless with or about our lives, but that we should care less about the situations in our lives and care more about the powerful influence of our heavenly Father and His great plans for us expressed in His promises in the pages of the scriptures. Now, let's take it further with this: should we have God-sanctioned plans? Yes, of course. Should we have strategies crafted and drafted under the

Holy Spirit's guidance? Yes. But should we loose our sleep and peace, wondering how our plans and strategies would work out? Shhh! Before giving an emphatic 'No' for an answer, Peter beckons on us as he reckons with Jesus' teaching on worry:

Casting all your care upon Him, for He cares for you (1 Peter 5:7). The effects of Jesus words must have been tremendous in the life of Peter to have made him use the same word Jesus used for 'worry' in describing 'care'. Matthew 6:25 in the Old King James Version puts 'worry' as 'taking thoughts'. It means to be anxious – the root of which is to disunite, to divide, to give apart. So, we have meanings of worry that do not only reveal what it implies, but also the impact it creates. In essence, when we become anxious, our minds, values and loyalties become divided and fragmented. Could this be the reason we cannot be full of worry and be full of faith at the same time? Or can our hearts be filled with myriads of anxious thoughts and be filled with trust and confidence in our Father's strength at the same time? Now, the question comes to us: what do we do with our worries and anxieties?

Again, Peter, remembering his escapades in his previous career pulls out his encyclopedia in Fishing from a dusty shelf on a windy Jewish afternoon. "We can drop our care at His feet?"… No. Drop will not really convey his intentions in this matter. "We can carry our care to Him?"… No. This would mean we can bear them before handing them over to God. Or this: "we can roll them over to?"… No. Not this. But… Yes! He eventually finds the word. He had probably exhibited this word in his lifetime more than a toddler had struggled finding his steps.

Casting all your care upon Him, for He cares for you (1 Peter 5:7). Fishermen are known to cast their nets into water bodies after which the nets are drawn to sort out the harvest of fishes. To cast means to 'throw into'. But Peter meant more than this in his choice of words. The root of the word 'casting' in 1 Peter 5:7 means 'to properly fling with a quick toss'. Let's do a prompt substitution of words and read the verse again: properly and quickly fling (throw) your care on Jesus (with a quick toss), for He cares for you. It is not enough to throw our worries on Jesus, but to also do so quickly. That is immediately the worrying and anxious thoughts creep into our hearts, they should be properly and quickly thrown over to Jesus. We should do this because our hearts and minds were not crafted to bear these pressures as Jesus is our burden-bearer. The One who bore the cross for us knows how to help us navigate the cross-roads of life. The heart that bore our guilts and shame knows how to fill our hearts with His joy and peace. The hands that designed our hearts know how to stabilize them with the power of His word. Let's build a castle of pneumonic with the word 'cast' so as not to lose track of it as we tread further.

C – Call on the Father. "Call upon me in the day of trouble; I will deliver you and you will give me glory" (Psalm 50:15).

A – Allow God to handle things in His own way. "Be still and know that I am God..." (Psalm 46:10). "In returning and rest, you shall be saved; in quietness and confidence, you shall be strengthened" (Isaiah 30:15); "He has made all things beautiful in His time" (Ecclesiastes 3:11).

S – Stay with His word. Read His word. Memorize His word. Study His word. Meditate on His word. Believe His word. Confess His word. Walk in His word. "Remember your word to your servant, upon which you have caused me to hope" (Psalm 119:49).

T – Trust Him with all confident assurance that He will always act in your favour. "Trust in the Lord with all your heart and lean not on your own understanding; in all your ways acknowledge Him and He will direct your paths" (Proverbs 3:5).

Let's take a little moment to savour the aura of hope in the castle of C-A-S-T as we reiterate what we do when we cast our cares on Jesus:

Call on the Father; Allow God to handle things in His own way; Stay with His word; Trust Him all the way.

Jaden decided to cast his cares on his father's shoulders and in the end, we were both happy. May we find the strength to trust our heavenly Father with every detail of our lives.

CHAPTER 3

THE FLAMES OF THE GAME

Her heart is heavy and her abdomen is enlarged. Her sighs are filled with anticipations and her expectations mixed with shallow frustrations. She has waited for this day all her life, but her picture of today as tomorrow, yesterday defies her present realities. Drenched in sweat, she wears an appearance of an Olympic athlete in the height of a training session, but for her protruded belly. The events of the previous months have taken their toll on her, climaxing with the challenging moments of the last few days. As the sun reclines into the shadow of the moon, she thinks of the journey that brought her here.

The process of a vision is like that of a pregnancy. First is the desire, then the conception followed by the trimesters. The first trimester is the period of cellular division and organ development. It is the time shredded ideas find a commonplace in the mind of an individual. It is the period hope mixes with faith in courageous anticipations despite obvious limitations.

The second trimester is the period of further growth and development. Conceived ideas develop with increased mastery of skills with personal and co-operate development. Here, character is further built with heightened insight into the understanding of purpose.

The third trimester is the period of expectations and performance. It is the time when all the incubating preparations and silent sacrifices turn into monumental delivery of visions into reality. In the third trimester, the mother's attention is focused on the day of delivery. "How will the baby look?", she asks herself.

The scream of Mary amidst the cry of her newborn aligns our hearts with our course. Mary brought forth her beloved child despite prevailing oppositions. Roses among thorns. Gold amidst coal. Starlight in a dark cloud. Here's the diamond found: going for the visions in our hearts despite roaring oppositions is a major step in the fulfillment of purpose in life. Apostle Paul did well when he admonished young Timothy:

You therefore must endure hardship as a good soldier of Jesus Christ.

No one engaged in warfare entangles himself with the affairs of this life, that he may please him who enlisted him as a soldier

And also if anyone competes in athletics, he is not crowned unless he competes according to the rules (2 Timothy 2:3-5).

Talk about rules of engagement and your point will soar with icons of relevance. Believers in Christ are soldiers, positioned to fulfill God's purpose in Christ Jesus. The fulfillment of purpose in life is like a warfare believers in Jesus have been enlisted in by the Lord Himself, who is the Captain that calls the shots. Take a deep breath. Recline your seat. Adjust your posture. The reason? You may need to read some words again. Perhaps Timothy did the same when he first received them:

"No one engaged in warfare entangles himself with the affairs of this life, that he may please Him who enlisted him as a soldier" (2 Timothy 2:4). Carve this verse on a marble stone, memorize it or paint it on a canvass, none will be out of place as long as it remains a mission statement in the event of purpose fulfillment. So, we cannot afford to be distracted by the happenings around us if we would be fully focused on the visions in our hearts.

Let's give the word 'entangle' a warm embrace of acceptance. In the context used, entangle means entwine, involve with. It means to become twisted together with, entrapped or caught in. In essence, if we are engaged in the fight for the fulfillment of purpose, we cannot afford to be entrapped or twisted together with the affairs of this life otherwise, we would not have succeeded in delivering the goals to please our Master who enlisted us in His eternal army. The affairs of this life are the distractions around us. They are the noise of clanging cymbals without melodies, the roaring of thunders without rain, and the deep wells without waters. They are the flare for fame, the lust for wealth, the unhealthy desires for power, positions and public affirmations. At other times, they show up as hardships, afflictions, limitations and rejections. The expired rent. The low gas.

The red account. The failed exam. What do we do when faced with the enticing or distressing vistas of affairs of this life? Apostle Paul smiles and gives a comforting nod:

And everyone who competes for the prize is temperate in all things. Now, they do it to obtain a perishable crown, but we for an imperishable crown. Therefore, I run thus: not with uncertainty. Thus I fight: not as one who beats the air (1 Corinthians 9:25-26).

All athletes practice strict self-control. They do it to win a prize that will fade away, but we do it for an eternal prize. So I run straight to the goal with purpose in every step. I am not like a boxer who misses his punches (1 Corinthians 9:25,26 NLT).

Let's harvest some words from the two versions for a cocktail of inspiration:

1. Strict self-control

2. Not with uncertainty

3. I run straight to the goal with purpose in every step

4. I fight not as one who beats the air

5. I am not like a boxer who misses his punches

Five great statements to note and ponder on. Five smooth layers of cushion to fall on when fatigued from the vicissitudes of life. Five prongs of the anchor of strength on the sail of purpose. Won't it be nice to find a word that unifies these five strong pillars? Here's a five-lettered word that can do the job – *focus*. Focus is the state or quality of having or producing clear visual definition. Focus is an attitude that has found relevance as a major strategy for excellence and productivity in all walks of life. From the three-pointer in a basketball game, the clinical finish in a soccer match, the successful performance of a procedure in a theatre, to the excellence of growing a nation's economy, the beauty of photography, the tenacity of consistency in Christian ministry, focus like sunshine is God's great gift to humanity. We need to be focused to run straight to the goal with purpose and fight without missing our punches. Focus will help us remain on track as we have our targets perfectly in view. Our focus should be ultimately on our Lord and Saviour, Jesus Christ because He is the object of our hope.

Looking unto Jesus, the author and finisher of our faith, who for the joy that was set before Him endured the cross, despising the shame, and has sat down at the right hand of the throne of God (Hebrews 12:2).

We cannot be fully focused on the Lord Jesus and at the same time dance to the enticing beats of distractions around us. As we maintain our focus on the Lord Jesus in continuous fellowship with Him, we will find strength to forge ahead as He is revealed to us by the Holy Spirit.

Here's a loud whisper: let's shift our focus to the next chapter.

CHAPTER 4

THE SOUND OF THE GAME

They've stayed on their jobs for quite a long time; longer they've now stayed on the field. When the smiles of the dawn dripped as dew, they stayed. When the breath of the day walked away and twilight cried out, they stayed. When it rained, they stayed. When the thunder struck, they stayed. Talk about the diary of a Shepherd and they all retrieve their scrolls and feathered pens:

8am – 9am – Ensure the flock lacks nothing

9am – 11am – Make the flock feed and lie in green pastures

11am – 12 noon – Lead the flock through a safe path

12 noon – 2pm – Lead the flock to drink from still waters

2pm – 4pm – Lead the flock back home

Disclaimer: the rod and the staff to be used as appropriate.

Now there were in the same country Shepherds living out in the fields, keeping watch over their flock by night

For there is born to you this day in the city of David a Saviour, who is Christ the Lord

And they came with haste and found Mary and Joseph, and the Babe lying in a manger (Luke 2:10,11,16).

Now, here's a question for the green room before the limelight: why would God send an Angel to some Shepherds living out in the fields to announce the birth of His dear Son? Why would the Angel not go to the chief priest in the synagogue? Whatever happened to the scribes or other religious leaders whose hearts and lives were filled with pious sanctimony? Could it be because Jesus would later announce Himself as the good Shepherd? For whom did they abandon the flock when they yielded to the heavenly call? And why did the Angel came to them at night and not during the day? Maybe because the nature of sin had darkened the souls of men like the blackness of the night. We don't know all these, but we do know that the Shepherds were informed and they responded with haste. They must have been used to being prompt and resilient in the face of necessity.

They were on an 8-4 job with regular night shifts, but no designer blazers, expensive bags or exotic cars. They threaded the path of excellence with willing hearts of passion and fruitful hands of diligence. The last word just paid a fee for attention and requests for a great value in exchange. The Greek word for diligence is *spoude.* It literally means speed and by implication means dispatch eagerness; earnestness in business. It means to be business-like, dutiful. Diligence is an imperative attitude required for the fulfillment of God's purpose for our lives. It is our response to the upward pull of the divine drive. It is our waltz of meaning to the sonorous music of purpose. It is our affirmation to the revelation of who we are in Christ Jesus. Diligence is like a pleasant river with gentle and loyal tributaries. Let's be more diligent in exploring these tributaries:

1. Competence – this is the quality or state of having sufficient knowledge, judgment, skill or strength. Competence is a product of continuous and meticulous trainings and sacrifices. It is a result of

intentional investment for proficiency over every form of deficiency. Competence is the reason people don't settle for less and they don't dance to the tune of the average. The difference between a professional and an amateur is competence. It is the 'awe' that breathes her warmth over an entity that makes it 'awesome'.

2. Consistency – this is the steadfast adherence to the same principles, course or form. Consistency is the ability to maintain the right course of actions even when there is no applause from the gallery. Consistency gives the power to continue even when the results to be embraced are still ahead. It is the strength that makes demanding tasks enjoyable.

3. Courage – this is the mental or moral strength to venture, persevere and withstand danger, fear or

difficulty. Courage compels us to drive harder towards success even when faced with the seemingly intimidating noise of failure. With courage, our dispositions towards failures and successes become the same in this: they are both opportunities to see more, learn more, do more and become more.

4. Confidence – this is the quality of being certain of your abilities. The ride of competence driven by consistency on the wheels of courage will definitely arrive at the district of confidence. And for us believers in Christ, our confidence is not in our abilities, but in God's ability made available for us in Christ Jesus through the presence of the Holy Spirit.

Not that we are sufficient of ourselves to think of anything as being from ourselves, but our sufficiency is from God (2 Corinthians 3:5).

As we motion on the tarmac of purpose, let's recall an important signpost here: the attitude of diligence will cause the melodies of competence, consistency, courage and confidence to be heard. Apart from this paradigm of scaling up capacity, an imperative ingredient that will maintain the floodlight of purpose is character. Character is the display of moral or ethical quality by an individual. In biblical terms, a word that fits perfectly with it is virtue – moral excellence. Character is an undisputable ally in the highway of success and in the words of honourable men, whatever diligence does, character sustains. Let's sustain the momentum of this discussion as we turn to a different path. Matthew opens the front door, welcomes us into his warm hub and leads us into his magnificent library. A virtual experience might have sufficed, but the brilliance of the arrangement of the intellectual gems leaves the eyes for more and for the umpteenth time, a literary piece written against his name calls for attention. We may as well do well to open it:

For the kingdom of heaven is like a man travelling to a far country, who called his own servants and delivered his goods to them.

And to one he gave five talents, to another two, and to another one, to each according to his own ability, and immediately, he went on a journey.

Then he who had received the five talents went and traded with them and made another five talents.

And likewise he who had received two gained two more also.

But he who had received one went and dug in the ground, and hid his lord's money

Then he who had received the one talent came and said, 'Lord, I knew you to be a hard man, reaping where you have not sown, and gathering where you have not scattered seed

And I was afraid, and went and hid your talent in the ground. Look, there you have what is yours.'

But his lord answered and said to him, 'You wicked and lazy servant, you knew that I reap where I have not sown and gathered where I have not scattered seed.

'So you ought to have deposited my money with the bankers, and at my coming I would have received back my own with interest.

Therefore take the talent from him, and give it to him who has ten talents (Matthew 25:14-18, 24-28).

The parable is a good account of what the bible says of diligence and character. Gifts are usually given according to abilities (capacities) and the latter increase by the effective use of gifts and other resources through diligence. Diligence brings out the essence of productivity because when gifts are used (traded with), they yield more by producing greater capacities for more.

The reason the third servant hid and failed to use his talent is because he was afraid. The fear of failure. The fear of not measuring up to certain standards. The fear of uncertainty about what the gifts could deliver. His fear wrapped him up in a notorious embrace to produce laziness and wickedness of him. With his sense of futility and failure, he did what other lazy people do – he blamed his master for his woes and failed to take responsibilities for his actions and inactions.

Apart from being diligent, another point to note from the Shepherds is the power of relationships – yes, right relationships. Right relationships are conduits of dignity through which streams of purpose flow. From ancient times, relationships have been invaluable and inevitable struts through which villains rise. Joshua's relationship with Moses transformed his life and ministry, just as it did for Timothy when he walked with Paul, the Apostle.

He who walks with wise men will be wise, but the companion of fools will be destroyed (Proverbs 13:20).

The right relationships help us to see more, know more, do more and become more. They are hubs of rubies and niches of wealth.

But we have this treasure in earthen vessels, that the excellence of power may be of God and not of us (2 Corinthians 4:7).

God's ability is resident in earthen vessels (humans) as treasures, values, wisdom in the hearts of men and we become beneficiaries of these treasures as we develop the right relationships with the right set of people.

We've had so much to say in this chapter. Let's take

our relationship to a higher level in the next

chapter.

CHAPTER 5

THE NAME OF THE GAME

It's a beautiful day. The bright sky gently greeted the early morning breeze with a warm embrace of bliss and the eloquent aura of the sunshine. In the meantime, the lushness of the lawn was more appealing as beautiful butterflies danced for fame along colourful petals. Like the ripple effect in a water body, the brightness of the day resonated in the minds of people that even a shepherd's heart was stirred in hope. He steps into the sheepfold to ensure the completeness of the sheep. He calls out their names as he counts out loud: "Billy – one, Willy – two, Dave – three…"

But he who enters by the door is the shepherd of the sheep.

To him the door keeper opens, and the sheep hear his voice; and he calls his own sheep by name and leads them out.

And when he brings out his own sheep, he goes before them; and the sheep follow him, for they know his voice

"Yet they will by no means follow a stranger, but will flee from him, for they do not know the voice of strangers

I am the door. If anyone enters by me, he will be saved, and will go in and out and find pasture.

I am the good Shepherd; and I know my sheep, and am known by my own (John 10:3-5,9,14).

Jesus, without ambiguity introduces us to Himself and with every sense of clarity defines His role in our lives. He is the door to the sheepfold of God's righteousness. We enter into the kingdom of God through His love and grace expressed in the death and resurrection of Jesus. In His kingdom, we have all that we need because of the riches of His grace.

He is our Shepherd. No! Sorry, that was a sharp blunder. He is more than a Shepherd to us – He is a good Shepherd, our good Shepherd. Jesus carefully chose His words when He said "I am the good Shepherd…" (John 10:4). The word 'good' as used in the context means beautiful, virtuous or valuable. So, we have a Shepherd who is beautiful, valuable and virtuous. His presence in our lives adds to us beauty and goodness. Our lives are valuable and filled with virtue because of Jesus, our good Shepherd. The identity and dignity of the sheepfold is in the strength and integrity of the Shepherd, hence the presence of Jesus in our lives bestows on us His goodness and beauty. Also, we have a wonderful Shepherd who calls us by name and leads us out for game. Isn't it amazing to know that we have a Shepherd who calls us by name and leads us personally and individually? He fashioned our hearts, designed our lives and leads us in unique ways according to His specific purpose and plans for us. He goes before us to show us the path of life, the ways of grace to embrace and the detours to avoid because He Himself is the Way. If these are His roles in our lives, shouldn't we have a part in all of these? Matthew cuts in and narrates an interesting story:

Now after six days Jesus took Peter, James and John his brother, led them on a high mountain by themselves;

And He was transfigured before them. His face shone like the sun, and His clothes became as white as the light

And behold, Moses and Elijah appeared to them, talking with Him.

Then Peter answered and said to Jesus, "Lord it is good for us to be here; if You wish, let us make here three tabernacles: one for you, one for Moses, and one for Elijah."

While he was still speaking, behold, a bright cloud overshadowed them; and suddenly a voice came out of the cloud saying, "This is My beloved Son, in whom I am well pleased. Hear Him!" (Matthew 17:1-5).

The brightness of the transfigured Christ dispelled the darkness of the wrongly-configured minds. The shining of His face was in similitude of the sunlight, even as the colour of His cloth was replaced by the whiteness of the light. This was Christ in an amazement that was never seen before and a wonder that was never experienced before. It was Christ in His purely divine and celestial form. In his innocent, yet incorrect view, Peter advised that three tabernacles be built to house Jesus, Moses and Elijah. That is, Jesus would be put in the same class with Moses and Elijah, but the Father interrupted him and declared "...hear Him." The law and the prophets that Moses and Elijah respectively represented pointed towards Jesus. Hear Him! Now, we are to hear all that Jesus came to say and do in redemption. Jesus is God's word personified. All that the Father has to say is in Jesus because all that the Father has to say is Jesus. The law and the prophets were necessary deals, but Jesus is the real deal – the only deal! As Peter later found out, we'd realize we dare not put the immortal God on the same pedestal with mortal men. Although Jesus is our Saviour, He is also our God and not only is He our Shepherd, He is also our King. Peter would later write with more understanding on this:

For He received from God the Father honour and glory when such a voice came to Him from the Excellent Glory: "This is My beloved Son, in whom I am well pleased."

And we heard this voice which came from heaven when we were with Him on the Holy mountain.

And so we have the prophetic word confirmed, which you do well to heed as a light that shines in a dark place, until the day dawns and the morning star rises in your hearts (2 Peter 1:17-19).

We are to heed everything Jesus says until every fibre and every detail of our lives becomes illuminated and absorbed by the word of God! We cannot know the voice of someone we have not heard. We know His voice in the place of His word, prayers and the revelation of His will. His responsibility is to call and lead us; our responsibility is to know and follow His voice. May our steps continuously be in line with the voice of our Shepherd. GRACE

<u>EPILOGUE</u>

Information and communication technology stepped into the world and our lives and experiences witnessed some drastic transformation. In one of the pictures used as display picture on some social media applications, a big cat is seen looking into the mirror. Interestingly, instead of seeing its own reflection, it sees that of a big lion, or fitly put, it sees itself as a lion. Wherever you are in the world,

stand beside a fireplace, switch on a heater in your room,
pick a glass of cold water as you sit, recline your sit if you
can, but don't ever go away without giving an honest
answer to the next question – what do you see, when you
see?

*But friends, that's exactly who we are: children of God.
And that's only the beginning. Who knows how we'll end
up! What we know is that when Christ is openly revealed,
we'll see him – and in seeing him, become like him. All of
us who look forward to his coming stay ready, with the
glistening purity of Jesus' life as a model for our own (1
John 3:2,3 MSG).*

Do you see that? Now, we are the children of God
because we have the abiding presence of the Holy Spirit
within us. The Holy Spirit reveals Jesus to us so that we

can see Him and become like Him in a greater level of glory and power. The image of Christ is the real definition of who we are and that is what we see when we get a revelation of Him through constant fellowship with Him from His word, prayers and worship.

But we all, with unveiled face, beholding as in a mirror the glory of the Lord, are being transformed into the same image from glory to glory, just as by the Spirit of the Lord (2 Corinthians 3:18).

The spotlight is on Jesus and the actual depth of our purpose is found in the full expression of whom Christ is, which comes to us through the revelation of Christ Himself by the Holy Spirit. Therefore, we are so privileged and at a great vantage position in Christ Jesus because our Saviour, Shepherd, King, Captain and Standard Definition is Christ Jesus Himself. We cannot do lesser than reflect

His love, life, power, glory and dominion, even as we

follow Him and walk in the fullness of His purpose for us.

Only in Christ is our purpose defined, revealed and

expressed! What do you think?

<u>ABOUT THE AUTHOR</u>

Loved by God to be a lover of God, Abolaji Paul Adekeye is

a Consultant Psychiatrist, a Mental Health Researcher,

Promoter and Advocate. A prolific writer, he has

publications in international peer reviewed journals and

has authored 2 Christian inspirational books, BRUISES and UNFAMILIAR PATHS.

He is an ordained minister at the Redeemed Christian Church of God where he serves as a Sunday School teacher and the Church secretary at the local church in Ado-Ekiti, Southwest Nigeria. He is passionate about revealing the grace of God, expressed in Christ Jesus through sound biblical teaching.

He is married to Oluwabusayo Adekeye who is a Lawyer, a gospel singer and the CEO of an excellent cake business. They have two sons together.

ABOUT THE BOOK

What does redemption in Christ has to do with the fulfillment of God's purpose for our lives? Everything. From the cradle in the manger through the struggle on the Romans' cross, the prophetic pendulum of the Father's purpose dangles in Christ Jesus and resonates for us every moment. And with the enlightenment that comes with the revelation of Jesus, we can willingly step into the reality of His will through the power of His grace.

REFERENCES

1. Competence. Merriam-Webster Dictionary [Internet].

2022[cited 2022 Mar 22]; Available online from:

https://www.merriam-

webster.com/dictionary/competence

2. Consistency. Dictionary.com [Internet]. 2022[cited 2022 Mar 22]; Available online from:

https://www.dictionary.com/browse/consistency

3. Courage. Merriam-Webster Dictionary [Internet]. 2022[cited 2022 Mar 22]; Available online from:

https://www.merriam-webster.com/dictionary/courage

4. Confidence. Cambridge Dictionary [Internet]. 2022[cited 2022 Mar 22]; Available online from:

https://dictionary.cambridge.org/dictionary/english/confidence

5. Character. Dictionary.com [Internet]. 2022[cited 2022 Mar 22]; Available online from:

https://www.dictionary.com/browse/character